U.S.A. TRAVEL GUIDES

GEORGIA

BY ANN HEINRICHS • ILLUSTRATED BY MATT KANIA

The Child's World®
childsworld.com

Published by The Child's World®
1980 Lookout Drive • Mankato, MN 56003-1705
800-599-READ • www.childsworld.com

Photo Credits

Photographs©: ESB Professional/Shutterstock Images, cover, 1; Shutterstock Images, 7, 31,38 (top), 38 (bottom); TimothyJ CC2.0, 8; Curtis Abert CC2.0, 11; Ron Cogswell CC2.0, 12; muffinn CC2.0, 15; Jared CC2.0, 16; Carol M. Highsmith Archive/Library of Congress, 19; Historic American Buildings Survey/Historic American Engineering Record/Historic American Landscapes Survey/Library of Congress, 20, 23; Karl Schumacher/Library of Congress, 22; Georgia Peanut Commission CC2.0, 24; muffinn CC2.0, 27; John Bazemore/AP Images, 28; Erik S. Lesser/EPA/Newscom, 32; JHP Attractions/Alamy, 35

ISBN 9781503819504
LCCN 2016961127

Printing

Printed in the United States of America
PA02334

Ann Heinrichs is the author of more than 100 books for children and young adults. She has also enjoyed successful careers as a children's book editor and an advertising copywriter. Ann grew up in Fort Smith, Arkansas, and lives in Chicago, Illinois.

About the Author
Ann Heinrichs

Matt Kania loves maps and, as a kid, dreamed of making them. In school he studied geography and cartography, and today he makes maps for a living. Matt's favorite thing about drawing maps is learning about the places they represent. Many of the maps he has created can be found in books, magazines, videos, Web sites, and public places.

About the
Map Illustrator
Matt Kania

On the cover: The Tallulah River winds through Tallulah Gorge.

OUR GEORGIA TRIP

Y ou're in for a great trip through Georgia! Just follow the dotted line—or else skip around. Either way, get ready for lots of fun.

You'll meet alligators and sea turtles. You'll build a wild and crazy peanut butter sandwich. You'll take a belly flop in the mud. And you'll even be a TV news reporter.

There's plenty more to do in Georgia. So buckle up, and let's hit the road!

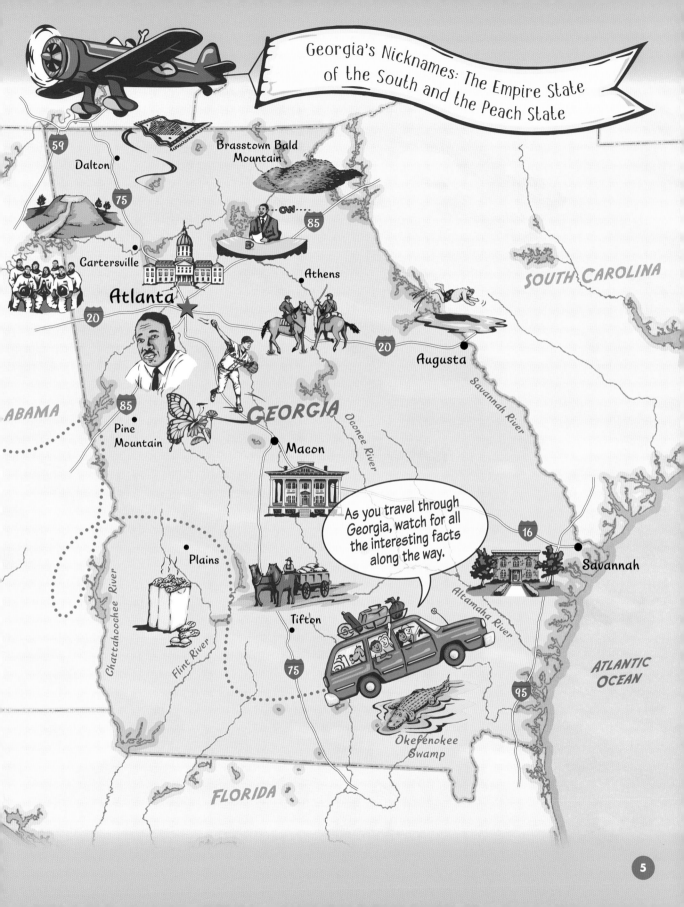

BRASSTOWN BALD MOUNTAIN

Take a hike up Brasstown Bald Mountain. It's Georgia's highest peak. There's a tower on the top. Climb up and look around. You can see North Carolina and South Carolina! They're states that border Georgia.

Northern Georgia is in the Appalachian Mountains. This region has many hills and valleys. South of the mountains is the Piedmont Region. It has low, rolling hills.

Southeastern Georgia faces the Atlantic Ocean. Islands called the Sea Islands lie offshore. One of the largest islands is Cumberland Island.

Okefenokee Swamp is in southeastern Georgia. It's a vast wetland. It's not all wet, though. Okefenokee contains many islands, grasslands, and small forests.

Brasstown Bald Mountain is the highest peak in the North Georgia Mountains.

OKEFENOKEE SWAMP

Your canoe glides along silently. Lacy **Spanish moss** hangs down from the trees. An alligator naps on the shady bank. Long-legged birds wade nearby.

You're in Okefenokee Swamp. Thousands of animals make their homes here. Crabs and giant turtles live along the coast. They're found on the Sea Islands, too.

Many animals live in the forests and mountains north of the swamp. Deer and bears are the largest. Smaller animals include foxes and raccoons.

Forests cover more than half the state. Pine and oak trees are common. Huge, sweet-smelling flowers bloom on Georgia's magnolia trees.

Canoe through lily pads, and keep an eye out for interesting wildlife at Okefenokee Swamp.

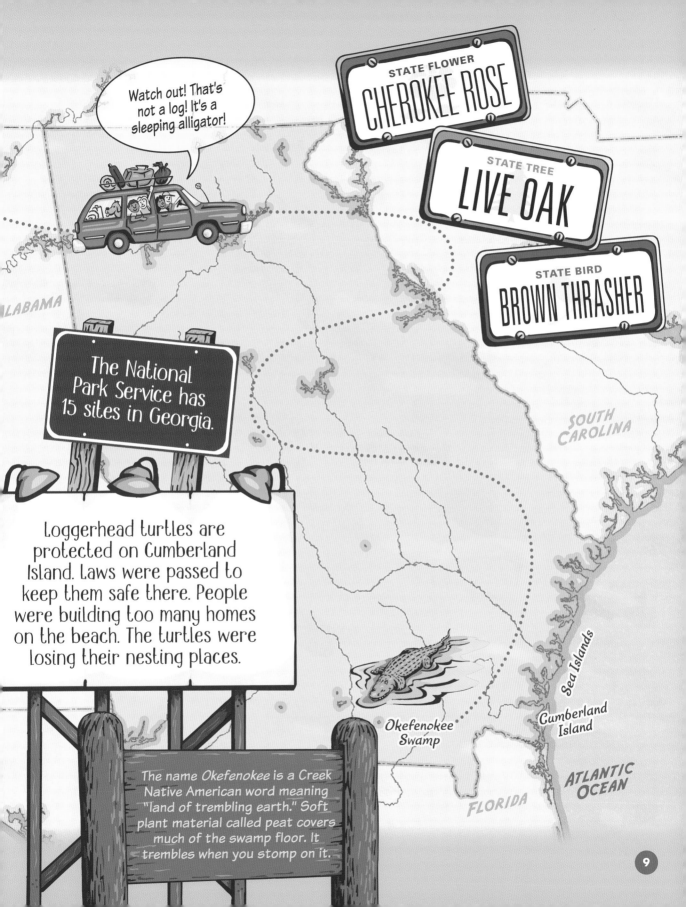

STATE FLOWER
CHEROKEE ROSE

STATE TREE
LIVE OAK

STATE BIRD
BROWN THRASHER

Watch out! That's not a log! It's a sleeping alligator!

The National Park Service has 15 sites in Georgia.

Loggerhead turtles are protected on Cumberland Island. Laws were passed to keep them safe there. People were building too many homes on the beach. The turtles were losing their nesting places.

The name *Okefenokee* is a Creek Native American word meaning "land of trembling earth." Soft plant material called peat covers much of the swamp floor. It trembles when you stomp on it.

ALABAMA

SOUTH CAROLINA

Sea Islands

Okefenokee Swamp

Cumberland Island

FLORIDA

ATLANTIC OCEAN

TENNESSEE

NORTH CAROLINA

SOUTH CAROLINA

Hurry up to the top! Then look out at that big **plaza**.

• Cartersville

The Ocmulgee National Monument near Macon contains Native American **artifacts**.

• Macon

Who Lived Here before Europeans Arrived? Mound Builders, Cherokee, and Muskogee (Creek)

ALABAMA

ATLANTIC OCEAN

The Creek Confederacy was a group of Native American tribes. It included the Muscogee (Creek). The tribes joined together to defend their territories.

More than 32,000 Native Americans live in Georgia today. Many are Cherokee or Creek.

The museum at Etowah Mounds displays tools, pottery, and statues. These items were found inside the mounds.

FLORIDA

ETOWAH MOUNDS AND GEORGIA'S EARLY PEOPLE

They look like big, flat-topped hills. But they were once part of a busy city. They are the Etowah Mounds in northwestern Georgia, near Cartersville.

Six huge mounds of earth stand in Etowah. Native Americans known as the Mississippians, or Mound Builders, built them approximately one thousand years ago. One mound had a temple on top. Others had homes on top or tombs inside.

The first Europeans arrived in Georgia in 1540. They were led by Spanish explorer Hernando de Soto. They carried diseases that spread to the Mound Builders. Many of the Mound Builders died. Others moved southwest into present-day Alabama. They became part of the Creek Confederacy.

Thousands of Native Americans once lived on the Etowah Mounds site.

OLD SAVANNAH'S PARKS

Welcome to Savannah's historic district. It looks like one big park!

Old Savannah is divided into more than 20 parks. These parks started out as public squares. They were surrounded by homes and businesses.

James Oglethorpe created Savannah's first city plan. He brought settlers from Great Britain in 1733. Their settlement grew into modern-day Savannah. This was the beginning of the Georgia **colony**. It was one of the 13 British colonies.

The colonies decided to fight for their freedom. They beat the British in the American Revolution (1775–1783). Then the colonies became the United States of America.

You will see beautiful fountains and flowers in Old Savannah's parks.

Georgia was named after King George II of Great Britain.

SOUTH CAROLINA

Let's splash in the fountain! Let's climb a tree!

Colonial leaders established a library in Savannah in 1736. In 1889, Dr. Francis T. Willis provided Georgia with its first free library.

ALABAMA

• Savannah

Juliette Gordon Low founded the Girl Scouts of America. Low was born in Savannah.

ATLANTIC OCEAN

James Oglethorpe led the first group of European settlers to Georgia. This group included 114 men, women, and children.

FLORIDA

Georgia was the fourth state to enter the Union. It joined on January 2, 1788.

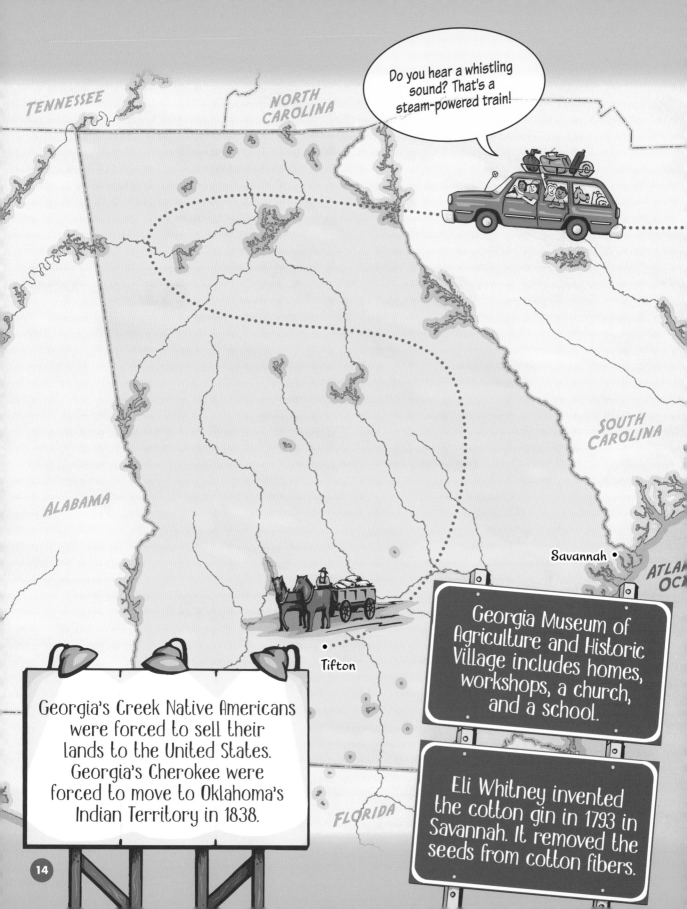

Chop, chop! The woodworker is busy. He's making a stool out of a tree stump. Clink, clink! The **blacksmith** hammers out horseshoes.

You're at the Georgia Museum of Agriculture and Historic Village in Tifton. It's a living-history town. People there live like **pioneers** did in the late 1800s.

Creek and Cherokee people have lived in Georgia for hundreds of years. But in the 1830s, they were forced onto reservations. Some were forced to sell their lands. Those who refused to sell their lands were forced out. Then many European settlers moved in. The settlers lived by farming. They made their own clothes, furniture, and tools.

Cotton became the leading crop in Georgia. Some people had cotton plantations, or large farms. African American people were often enslaved to work on these plantations.

See an old printing press at the Georgia Museum of Agriculture's print shop.

THE ATLANTA HISTORY CENTER

Men stand stiffly in uniforms. You see a tent and camping equipment. Did you wander into a military camp? No! You are at the Atlanta History Center. Those men are wax figures. They are models of Confederate and Union soldiers from the Civil War (1861–1865).

The Confederacy was made up of several Southern states. One of them was Georgia. These states pulled away from the Union. Confederate states wanted to keep slavery. But Union states wanted to end it. The two sides fought each other in the Civil War.

Union general William Sherman marched through Georgia. He destroyed buildings in his path. He burned Atlanta and captured Savannah. Finally, the Union won the war. Then the enslaved people were freed. But it was a long road to equality.

Step back in time, and learn more about the Civil War at the Atlanta History Center.

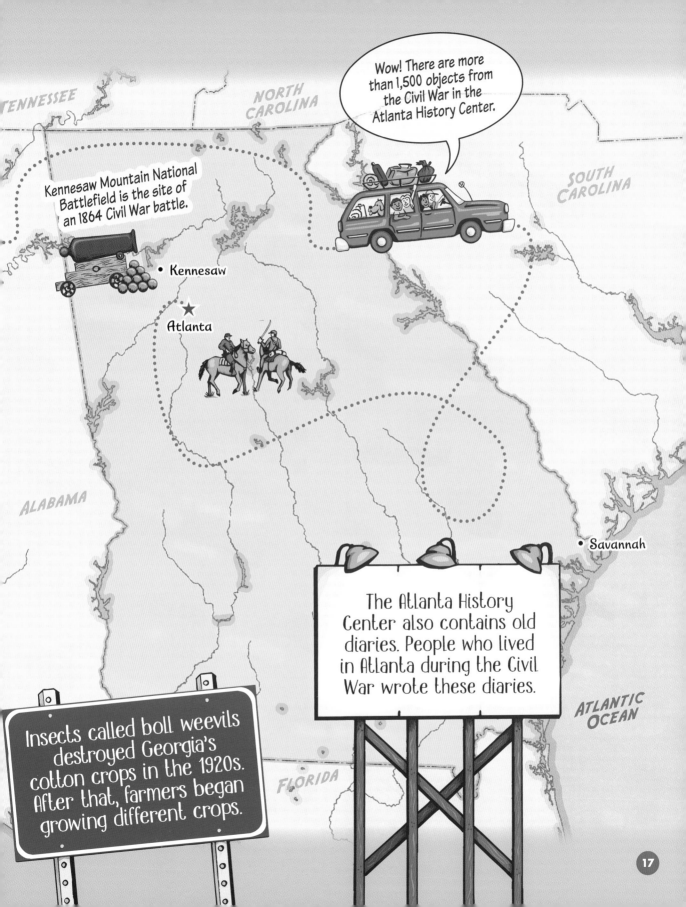

Wow! There are more than 1,500 objects from the Civil War in the Atlanta History Center.

Kennesaw Mountain National Battlefield is the site of an 1864 Civil War battle.

TENNESSEE

NORTH CAROLINA

SOUTH CAROLINA

• Kennesaw

★ Atlanta

ALABAMA

• Savannah

The Atlanta History Center also contains old diaries. People who lived in Atlanta during the Civil War wrote these diaries.

ATLANTIC OCEAN

Insects called boll weevils destroyed Georgia's cotton crops in the 1920s. After that, farmers began growing different crops.

FLORIDA

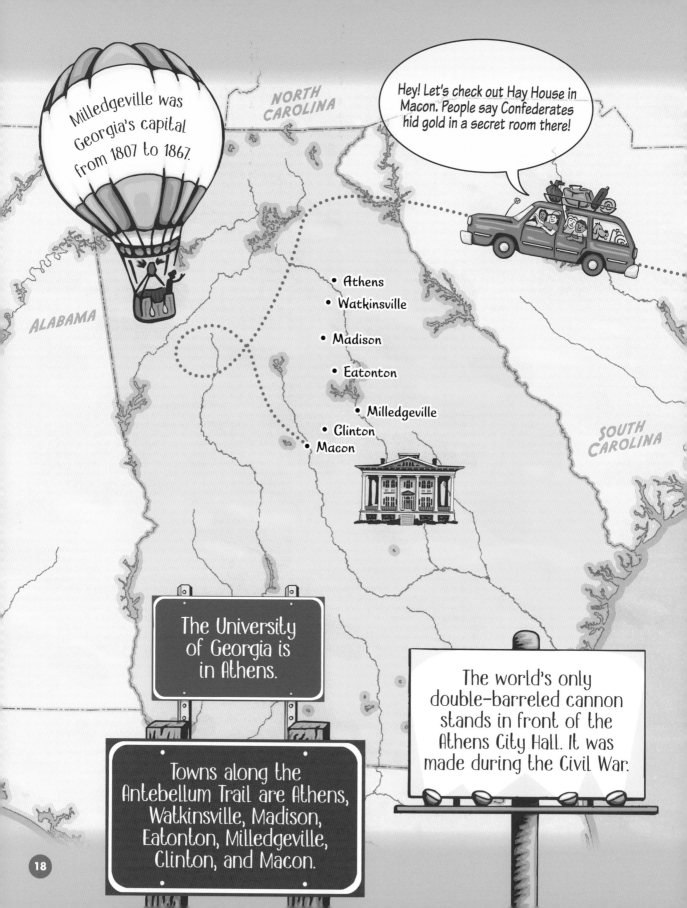

THE ANTEBELLUM TRAIL

Take a drive along Georgia's Antebellum Trail. It's like taking a trip back in time. *Antebellum* means "before the war." In this case, it refers to the time before the Civil War.

Seven towns lie along the Antebellum Trail. They stretch from Athens to Macon. These towns survived the Civil War.

General Sherman did not burn them down.

Lots of old **mansions** stand along the trail. Many are more than 150 years old. They have tall columns on their front porches. Some have beautiful gardens. Graceful magnolia trees shade the lawns. You'll find many other historic sites along the trail.

The Hay House mansion in Macon is a popular place to visit. You'll find it along the Antebellum Trail.

Martin Luther King Jr. was born in Atlanta. He and his family lived in his grandparents' home. The two-story house stands on Auburn Avenue.

Ebenezer Baptist Church is right down the street. King's father and grandfather were ministers there. Ministers are church officials who lead services and preach. King became a minister, too.

King also became a hero for many people. He worked to gain equal rights for African Americans. He also preached about peace and working together.

Today, King's neighborhood is a national historic site. Take a walk down the quiet streets. King walked there as a child. Even then, he probably had big ideas on his mind!

Tour Dr. King's home in Atlanta to learn more about his childhood.

Check out the King Center. You can hear King's "I Have a Dream" speech there.

African American and white students in Georgia once had to attend separate schools.

NORTH CAROLINA

SOUTH CAROLINA

★ Atlanta

Dr. King was awarded the 1964 Nobel Peace Prize.

ALABAMA

Dear Dr. King:
You gave a speech called "I Have a Dream." You dreamed of equal rights for everyone. Thanks to you, Congress passed the Civil Rights Act of 1964. Way to go, Dr. King!

Sincerely,
Selma Montgomery

post card

Dr. Martin Luther King Jr.
1929-1968
Atlanta, GA

Julian Bond was an African American civil rights leader. He served in Georgia's General Assembly (1967-1987).

FLORIDA

ATLANTIC OCEAN

Maynard Jackson became the first African American mayor of Atlanta in 1973.

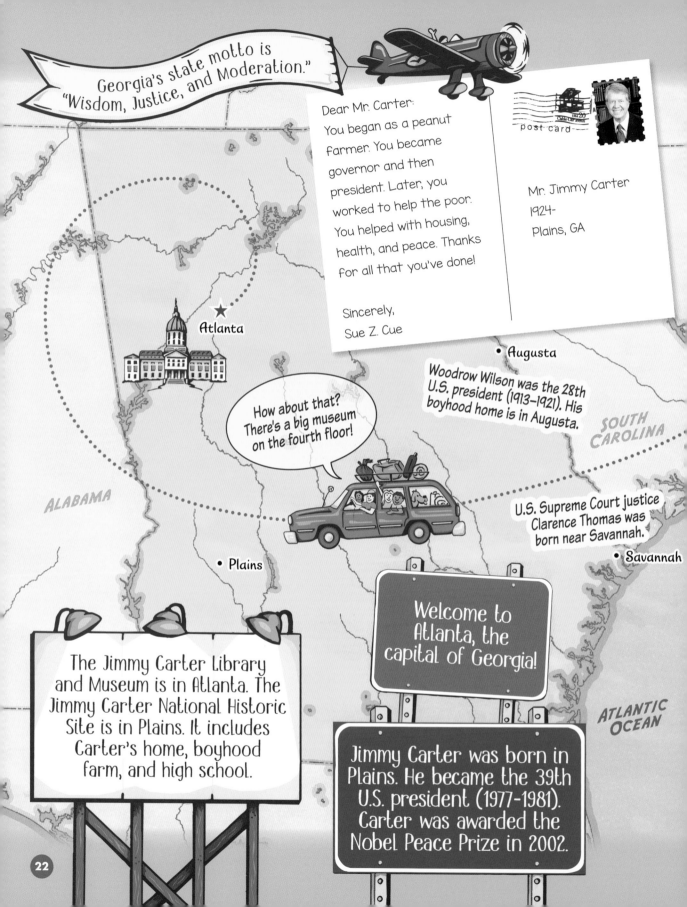

Georgia's state motto is "Wisdom, Justice, and Moderation."

Dear Mr. Carter:
You began as a peanut farmer. You became governor and then president. Later, you worked to help the poor. You helped with housing, health, and peace. Thanks for all that you've done!

Sincerely,
Sue Z. Cue

post card

Mr. Jimmy Carter
1924-
Plains, GA

Atlanta

How about that? There's a big museum on the fourth floor!

• Augusta

Woodrow Wilson was the 28th U.S. president (1913-1921). His boyhood home is in Augusta.

SOUTH CAROLINA

ALABAMA

U.S. Supreme Court justice Clarence Thomas was born near Savannah.

• Plains

• Savannah

The Jimmy Carter Library and Museum is in Atlanta. The Jimmy Carter National Historic Site is in Plains. It includes Carter's home, boyhood farm, and high school.

Welcome to Atlanta, the capital of Georgia!

ATLANTIC OCEAN

Jimmy Carter was born in Plains. He became the 39th U.S. president (1977-1981). Carter was awarded the Nobel Peace Prize in 2002.

THE STATE CAPITOL IN ATLANTA

Stroll up to the state capitol in Atlanta. You might feel like you've seen it before. It's built to look like another famous building. Can you guess which one? The nation's capitol in Washington, DC!

Inside Georgia's capitol are many state government offices. The state government has three branches. One branch makes the state's laws. It's called the General Assembly. Another branch carries out the laws. The governor heads this branch. The third branch is made up of judges. They decide whether laws have been broken.

The people of Georgia donated the gold that was used to build the state capitol dome.

THE PLAINS PEANUT FESTIVAL

A person in a peanut costume waves at you. A van that looks like a giant peanut passes by on the street. Are you dreaming? No! You're watching a parade at the Peanut Festival in Plains.

Georgia's Plains Peanut Festival celebrates peanuts with a parade, races, and contests. Peanuts are an important crop in Georgia. Georgia grows more peanuts than any other state. It's the top producer of pecans, too.

Other important crops are cotton, tobacco, and peaches. Georgia is sometimes called the Peach State. Many Georgia farmers also raise cattle and hogs.

Get ready to eat lots of peanuts at the Plains Peanut Festival!

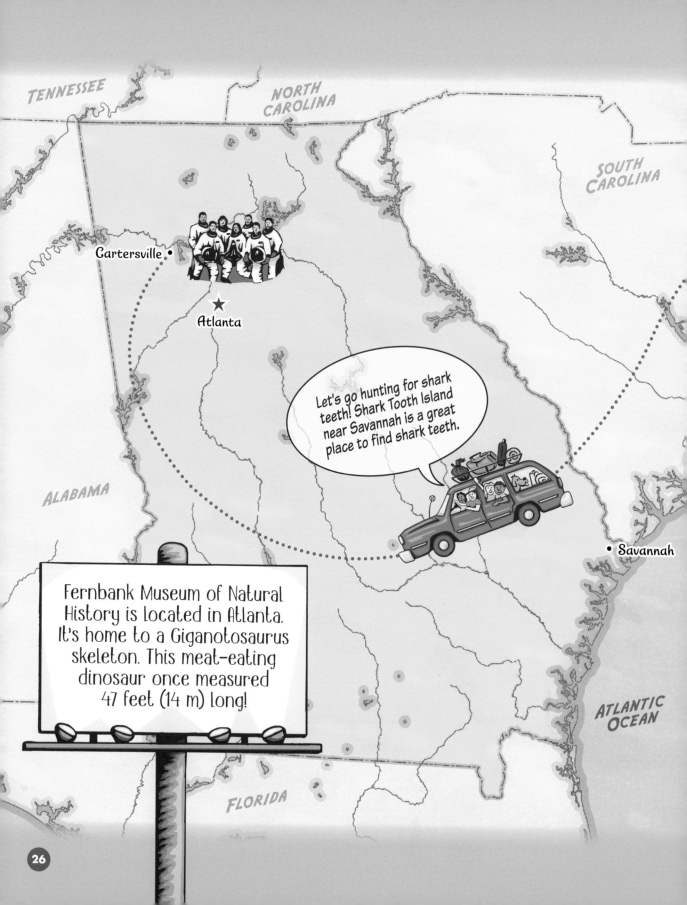

THE TELLUS SCIENCE MUSEUM IN CARTERSVILLE

See a moon rock. Step inside a model of a spacecraft. Dig for **fossils** and gems. You're at the Tellus Science Museum!

Would you like to be an astronaut? You can learn more about the solar system in the Tellus Science Museum's planetarium. A planetarium is a room with a curved ceiling. Images of stars and planets are projected onto the ceiling.

You can also see a megalodon jaw at the Tellus Science Museum. Megalodons were giant sharks. Millions of years ago, an ocean covered the land that is now Georgia. Megalodons swam in that ocean. It's good that they're not around anymore. Their jaws are taller than you!

See how you would look in a NASA spacesuit at the Tellus Science Museum.

DALTON'S CARPET MILLS

Machines are buzzing and humming. They spin and twist the carpet fibers. They dye the carpets many colors. At last, the carpets are sheared. That's like shaving them!

You're touring a carpet mill in Dalton. Dalton calls itself the Carpet Capital of the World. It makes more carpets than any other U.S. city.

Georgia sells its factory products all over the world. These include food, drinks, cars, and aircraft. Georgia makes medicines, paint, and paper, too.

Many people work at the carpet mills in Dalton.

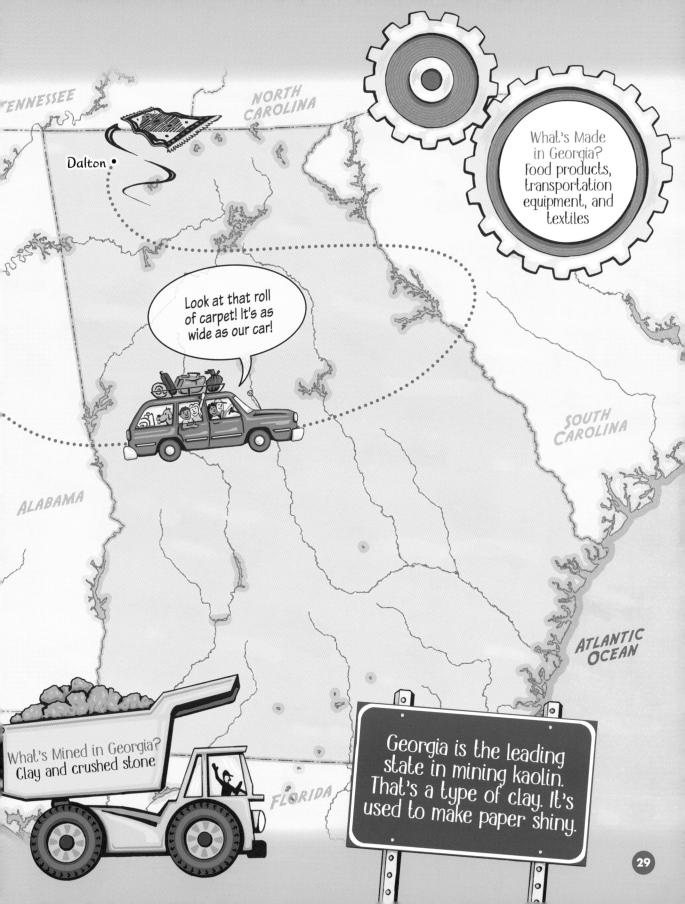

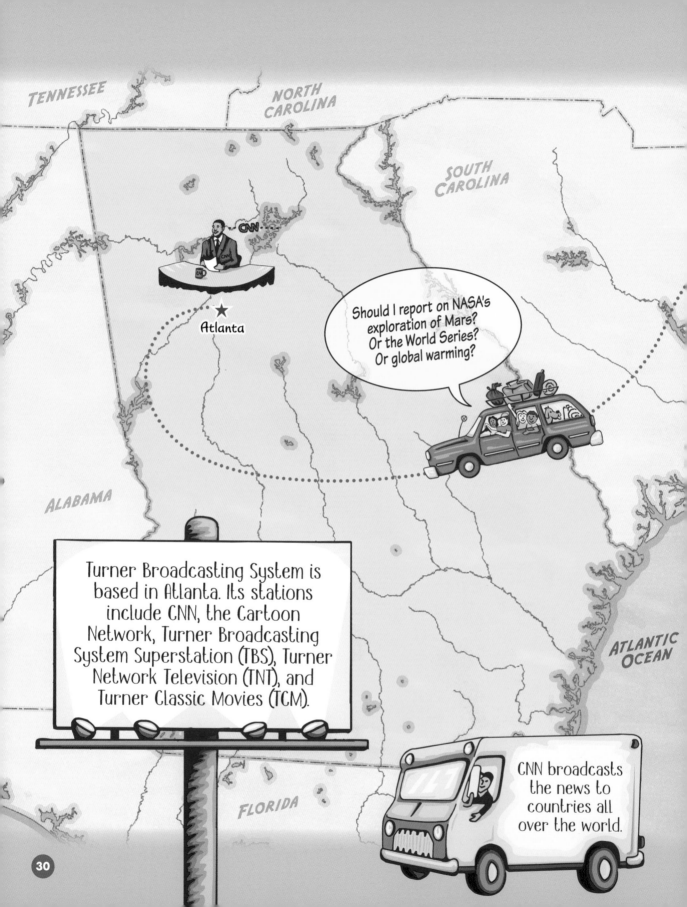

Should I report on NASA's exploration of Mars? Or the World Series? Or global warming?

Turner Broadcasting System is based in Atlanta. Its stations include CNN, the Cartoon Network, Turner Broadcasting System Superstation (TBS), Turner Network Television (TNT), and Turner Classic Movies (TCM).

CNN broadcasts the news to countries all over the world.

CNN STUDIOS IN ATLANTA

The cameras are rolling. You're seated at the **anchor** desk. And you're reporting today's top news stories!

You're touring the CNN studios in Atlanta. CNN stands for Cable News Network. While you wait for the tour, there's a special treat. You get to give your own news broadcast! You can get a video of your broadcast when you're done.

It's a great tour. You'll visit the control room. That's where news shows are put together. You'll find out how broadcasts are sent to viewers around the world. You'll stop by the special-effects department. There you'll see how TV weather maps appear.

The CNN Studios building is huge! There are many shops and restaurants to visit after your tour.

REDNECK GAMES AND OTHER FOLK TRADITIONS

Want to belly flop into a mud pit? Or race through a giant mud puddle? Just come to the annual National Redneck Games in Augusta!

Some Georgians like to say they're rednecks. That's a name for country people in the South. The National Redneck Games are all in fun. They celebrate some of Georgia's folk **traditions**. Quilt making and country music are Georgia traditions, too.

About three out of ten Georgians are African American. The Gullah are a special group of African Americans. They live on the Sea Islands and the coast. They have kept many of their African traditions. These include language, customs, crafts, and stories.

Be prepared to get messy at Georgia's National Redneck Games!

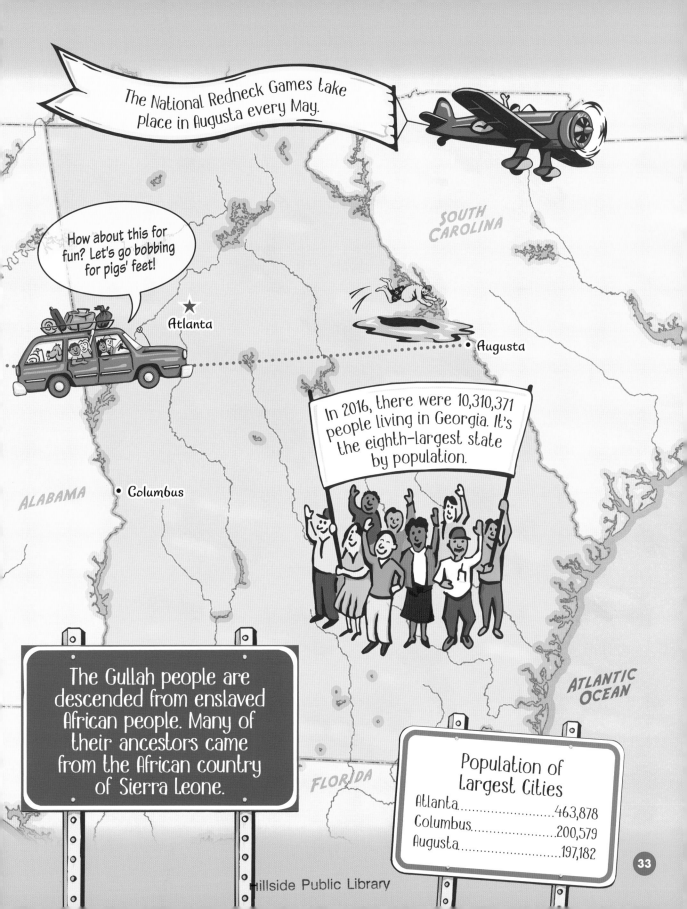

The National Redneck Games take place in Augusta every May.

How about this for fun? Let's go bobbing for pigs' feet!

SOUTH CAROLINA

★ Atlanta

• Augusta

ALABAMA

• Columbus

In 2016, there were 10,310,371 people living in Georgia. It's the eighth-largest state by population.

The Gullah people are descended from enslaved African people. Many of their ancestors came from the African country of Sierra Leone.

ATLANTIC OCEAN

FLORIDA

Population of Largest Cities
Atlanta........................463,878
Columbus....................200,579
Augusta.......................197,182

33

Hillside Public Library

TENNESSEE

NORTH CAROLINA

• Narrows

• Royston

Wow! The Georgia Sports Hall of Fame is the country's biggest state sports museum!

★ Atlanta

• Augusta

SOUTH CAROLINA

• Macon

The Tubman Museum is in Macon. It teaches people about African American art, history, and culture.

ALABAMA

The Georgia Sports Hall of Fame was built in 1956.

ATLANTIC OCEAN

Georgia Sports Teams
Atlanta Braves (baseball)
Atlanta Falcons (football)
Atlanta Hawks (basketball)

FLORIDA

Baseball champ Ty Cobb (1886-1961) was born in Narrows. He was a record-setting batter and base stealer. The Ty Cobb Museum is in Royston.

THE GEORGIA SPORTS HALL OF FAME IN MACON

In one room, you will find the uniforms of famous athletes. Walk into another room, and you can see a NASCAR car up close. You are in the Georgia Sports Hall of Fame. It is a must-see museum for sports fans. It houses thousands of artifacts from some of Georgia's best athletes.

Watching sports is a popular pastime in Georgia. Atlanta is home to several sports teams. Augusta is a famous city for golfers. That's where the Masters golf tournament is held.

Georgia is a great place to enjoy the outdoors. Some people like fishing or hiking in the woods. Others enjoy the seacoast. They're sure to meet seabirds, turtles, and crabs!

Learn about Georgia's sports history at the Georgia Sports Hall of Fame.

OUR TRIP

We visited many amazing places on our trip! We also met a lot of interesting people along the way. Look at the map below. Use your finger to trace all the places we have been.

What animals are protected on Cumberland Island? *See page 9 for the answer.*

Who was Georgia named after? *Page 13 has the answer.*

Who invented the cotton gin? *See page 14 for the answer.*

What towns are located along the Antebellum Trail? *Look on page 18 for the answer.*

Who was Julian Bond? *Page 21 has the answer.*

Where was former president Jimmy Carter born? *Turn to page 22 for the answer.*

What is kaolin? *Look on page 29 and find out!*

Who are the Gullah people? *Turn to page 32 for the answer.*

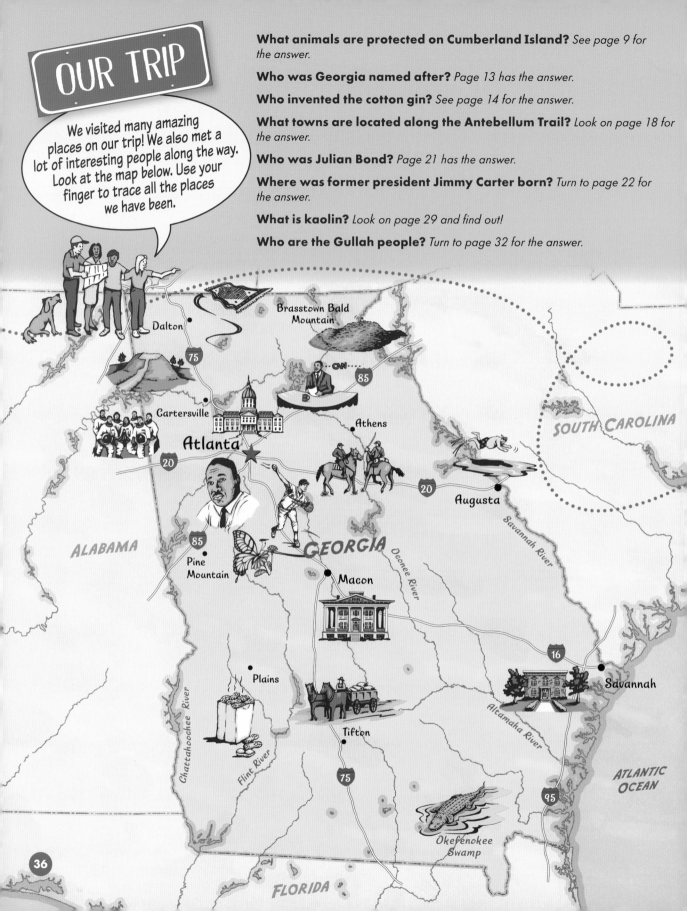

STATE SONG

"GEORGIA ON MY MIND"

Words by Stuart Gorrell, music by Hoagy Carmichael

Melodies bring memories
That linger in my heart
Make me think of Georgia
Why did we ever part?

Some sweet day when blossoms fall
And all the world's a song
I'll go back to Georgia
'Cause that's where I belong.

Georgia, Georgia, the whole day
   through
Just an old sweet song keeps Georgia on
   my mind.
Georgia, Georgia, a song of you
Comes as sweet and clear as moonlight
   through the pines.

Other arms reach out to me
Other eyes smile tenderly
Still in peaceful dreams I see
The road leads back to you.

Georgia, Georgia, no peace I find
Just an old sweet song keeps Georgia on
   my mind

STATE SYMBOLS

State art museum: Georgia Museum of Art

State bird: Brown thrasher

State butterfly: Eastern tiger swallowtail

State creed: Georgian's Creed

State crop: Peanut

State fish: Largemouth bass

State flower: Cherokee rose

State folk dance: Square dance

State folk festival: The Georgia Folk Festival

State fossil: Shark tooth

State fruit: Peach

State game bird: Bobwhite quail

State gem: Quartz

State insect: Honeybee

State marine mammal: Right whale

State mineral: Staurolite

State musical theater: Jekyll Island
Musical Theatre Festival

State reptile: Gopher tortoise

State seashell: Knobbed whelk

State theater: Springer Opera House

State transportation history museum:
Southeastern Railway Museum

State tree: Live oak

State vegetable: Vidalia sweet onion

State waltz: "Our Georgia"

State wildflower: Azalea

That was a great trip! We have traveled all over Georgia! There are a few places that we didn't have time for, though. Next time, we plan to visit the Cecil B. Day Butterfly Center in Pine Mountain. This conservatory features more than 1,000 tropical butterflies. Visitors can also view various tropical plants and birds.

FAMOUS PEOPLE

Aiken, Conrad (1889–1973), poet

Boynton, Amelia (1911–2015), civil rights activist

Carter, Jimmy (1924–), 39th U.S. president

Charles, Ray (1930–2004), singer

Cobb, Ty (1886–1961), baseball player

Felton, Rebecca Latimer (1835–1930), politician and writer

Hardy, Oliver (1892–1957), comedic actor

Hogan, Hulk (1953–), wrestler

Howard, Dwight (1985–), basketball player

King, Martin Luther, Jr. (1929–1968), civil rights leader

Knight, Gladys (1944–), singer

Low, Juliette Gordon (1860–1927), Girl Scouts founder

O'Connor, Flannery (1925–1964), author

Penniman, Richard "Little Richard" (1932–), singer

Redding, Otis (1941–1967), singer

Roberts, Julia (1967–), actor

Robinson, Jackie (1919–1972), baseball player

Thomas, Clarence (1948–), Supreme Court justice

Walker, Alice (1944–), author

Yearwood, Trisha (1964–), singer

State flag

WORDS TO KNOW

anchor (ANG-kur) a reporter who reads the news and introduces news reports

artifacts (ART-uh-fakts) objects that were used by human beings of the past

blacksmith (BLAK-smith) someone who makes metal objects using fire to heat the metal and a hammer to shape it

civil rights (SIV-il RITES) rights that all people in a nation should have

colony (KOL-uh-nee) a new land with ties to a parent country

fossils (FOSS-uhlz) remains or prints of plants or animals that have hardened into stone

mansions (MAN-shuhnz) huge, elegant houses

pioneers (pye-uh-NEERZ) people who settle in a new land

plaza (PLAH-zuh) a wide-open space with buildings around it

Spanish moss (SPA-nish MAWSS) a plant that grows on trees and has long, hanging vines

traditions (truh-DISH-uhnz) customs and ways of life handed down from generation to generation

State seal

TO LEARN MORE

IN THE LIBRARY

Cunningham, Kevin. *The Georgia Colony*. New York, NY: Children's Press, 2011.

Gregory, Josh. *Martin Luther King Jr*. New York, NY: Children's Press, 2015.

Naber, Therese. *Native Nations of the Southeast*. Mankato, MN: The Child's World, 2016.

Owings, Lisa. *Georgia*. Minneapolis, MN: Bellwether, 2014.

ON THE WEB

Visit our Web site for links about Georgia:
childsworld.com/links

Note to Parents, Teachers, and Librarians: We routinely verify our Web links to make sure they are safe and active sites. So encourage your readers to check them out!

PLACES TO VISIT OR CONTACT

Georgia Tourism and Travel
exploregeorgia.org
6000 N Terminal Parkway
Atlanta, GA 30320
800/847-4842
For more information about traveling in Georgia

Georgia Historical Society
georgiahistory.com
501 Whitaker Street
Savannah, GA 31401
912/651-2125
For more information about the history of Georgia

Georgia covers 59,425 square miles (153,910 sq km). It's the 24th-largest state in size.

INDEX

Bye, Empire State of the South. We had a great time. We'll come back soon!